The Story of  Odd Fellowship

By
Francis M. Dodge

Edited with a Suggested Reading List
By
Allison D. Bryant

Frankfort MI
C A Heritage
2013

Original Copyright
June 1, 1935
FRANCIS M. DODGE
116 Winona Ave.
Highland Park, Mich

ISBN-13:978-1490578439

ISBN-10:1490578439

============================

The story of Odd Fellowship is respectfully dedicated to the
officers of the Grand Lodge I. O. O. F. of Michigan
as an expression of appreciation of their un-tiring efforts in
behalf of the Order

---F. M. D.

======================

The Editor would like to express his appreciation to the Grand
Lodge F. & A. M. of Michigan and the Michigan Masonic
Museum and Library (John A. Wallsteadt, Director) for their
assistance.

---A. D. B.

CONTENTS

INTRODUCTION

The challenge of history is to recover the past and introduce it to the present. ~David Thelen

Seventy-eight years has passed since the author, Past Grand Master Francis Dodge (PGM of both the Grand Lodge of Michigan I.O.O.F and the Grand Lodge of Free and Accepted Masons of Michigan - the only man in Michigan to had this distinction) published this excellent history, and it still stands the test of time.

It should be noted that Brother Dodge received his Initiatory Degree in August 1934, his Scarlet Degree in October, 1935, was installed Vice Grand in 1936 AND managed to write the book you hold in your hand all in the same year. This is a demonstration of both his determination, abilities and devotion to the Order.

The world is much different than when Brother Dodge wrote this little tome. We have seen a second great world war, the cold war begin and end, wars in Vietnam, Korea and Iraq, nuclear weapons, personal computers and cell phones for every man, woman and child in the United State (or so it seems at times.)

As far as our gentle Order in Michigan is concerned, we have witnessed the change from having a Home in Jackson to Members Relief Endowment, the Sovereign Grand Lodge moving from Baltimore MD to Winston-Salem NC and, of course, women being admitted as Odd Fellows in all the branches. Our latest venture is the Odd Fellow Fraternal Museum in Litchfield, MI.

3

Brother Dodge's book is, word for word, as he wrote it in 1935, which for an editor is a challenge in itself. It is a very readable history and lacks the verbosity of many of the earlier histories of our Order. It is thorough and informative without the obvious flaw of being "preachy" or taking liberties with the facts as we know them.

Enjoy the book! While I never had the opportunity to meet Brother Dodge, I can sense some of his philosophy and dedication to Odd Fellowship within the pages of this volume.

St John's Day in Summer 2013

ADB

Francis M. Dodge
(1902 – 1993)

FRANCIS M. DODGE BIOGRAPHY

Brother Francis M. Dodge, Past Grand Master of the Grand Lodge (1948-49) and Past Grand Master of Masons in Michigan (1958-59) is the only man to have held positions of responsibility in both our fraternities.

Carlyle has said "history is the essence of innumerable biographies," thus it is fitting that we include an overview of Brother Dodge's life in this reprint of his 1935 history.

He was born at Manistee, Mich., Oct. 2, 1902, the son of Denton M. Dodge and Mary Louise Oudinot, and on his father's side is descended from a Scottish Presbyterian Elder who came to the United States early in the 18th century and settled on the St. Lawrence river in northern New York. His mother is a direct descendant of Field Marshal Oudinot, who was one of Napoleon's important aides.

Brothe Dodge received his early schooling in the grade and high schools of Manistee and received his higher learning in the Detroit City Law school, which is now part of Wayne University, being graduated therefrom in 1932 with an L.L.B. degree.

After graduation, he practiced as an attorney and counselor-law in Detroit. As an attorney he had been admitted to practice before all the Courts of Michigan as well as in other states, and before the Supreme Court of the United States of America.

Brother Dodge married, on Jan. 19, 1934, the charming Rita B. Codling, daughter of one of Royal Oak's early Mayors. Mrs. Dodge has long been associated with the Detroit Public School system and served as Principal of the Greenfield Union

School. The Dodges were members of the Methodist Church.

While active in his profession and in his fraternity, it we also know that he spent considerable time at play. His particular hobbies were fishing and golf, thus he fished occasionally in the north and in the south and played upon occasion what he termed "a lousy game of golf."

God has always endowed men with various gifts. In this instance, Brother Dodge possessed a gracious personality and a considerable store of wisdom. His charm of manner captivates and holds all who knew him. Learning and wisdom are his, yet withal he was humble and gentle with his fellowman-dislikes ostentation or arrogance -but enjoys a true pride in the heritage which was his.

The tradition of an Odd Fellow home with parents active for many years in the Order, gave Brother Dodge the background for an interesting career in Odd Fellowship. He was initiated into Benevolence Lodge No. 551, Detroit, on August 22, 1934, and received the Scarlet Degree October 5th of the same year. His profound interest in the Order and his Lodge was readily recognized as in January 1935 he was installed as Vice Grand of his Lodge and as Noble Grand the following term. He represented his Lodge in the Grand Lodge for the first time in 1936, and was subsequently assigned, to work on many of the important committees of the Grand Lodge.

In 1937 Brother Karl Keefer, Deputy Grand Master conceived the idea of an Odd Fellow Outdoor camp for boys, and with the consent of the Grand Master, Brother A. J. Brodie, he arranged for the services of a Methodist Camp near Vanderbilt, Michigan, where more than thirty' boys were entertained for a week as guests of Odd Fellows of Michigan. This project was officially recognized and sanctioned by the

7

Grand Lodge at the next session, and Brother Dodge was asked by the Grand Master to assume the responsibilities as chairman of a committee to handle the affairs of the "Camp".

At the 1938 session of the Grand Lodge,Brother Dodge introduced legislation to establish and maintain an Odd Fellow and Rebekah Camp for boys and girls as a Grand Lodge project. The legislation was adopted 'and Brother Dodge became the first President of the Camp Board of Control.

In December of 1938 a plan was presented to the Grand Lodge Officers by Brother Dodge which resulted in the adoption by the Grand Lodge of a Blood Donor program. Blood transfusions made possible' through this program saved many lives and brought relief to thousands of suffering individuals. Michigan Odd Fellowship gained international publicity through the work of this program.

Brother Dodge has always demonstrated a willingness and ,desire to be of utmost service to the Order. He was responsible for the legislation resulting in joint public ,installations of Grand Lodge and Rebekah Assembly officers in Michigan.

Brother Dodge was a member of Harland Lodge No. 56.5, Detroit; a Past Chief Patriarch of Enterprise Encampment No. 17, and of Home City Canton No. 463.

Brother Dodge's Masonic career began almost immediately after initiation and have never ceased. He was raised to the Sublime Degree of a Master Mason, Dee. 15, 1936, by Loyalty Lodge No. 488, Detroit.

In 1945 he served with distinction as Worshipful Master of his mother Lodge.

Always interested in the youth of our state, it was his legislation which, when adopted by Grand Lodge, permitted the Rainbow Girls and Job's Daughters to meet in Michigan Masonic Lodge Rooms.

He passed on to the Grand Lodge above on May 1, 1993.

Odd Fellowship

There has been for some time, on the part of many earnest and able members of our Order, a sincere desire to answer with a single statement the question so frequently asked, "What is Odd Fellowship?" None of the gentlemen have been able to prepare a declaration so concise, yet carrying such a wealth of information, as to embrace in one sentence a full and complete reply. Probably this can not be done. We must remember that in trying to define Odd Fellowship we are trying to define something that is intangible, something which is more "of the spirit than of the flesh."

Odd Fellowship is the practice of the principles of the Odd Fellows. The cardinal duties of an Odd Fellow are, "To visit the sick, relieve the distressed, bury the dead and educate the orphan." Note that we do not say the duty is to visit our brother Odd Fellows who are sick nor to relieve our brother Odd Fellows who are distressed. The command is general: to visit the sick where we find them, to relieve all such distress as we are able.

The fundamental idea of Odd Fellowship is charity as opposed to selfishness. The motto of the Odd Fellows perhaps expresses what Odd Fellowship is as comprehensively as words may express it-Friendship, Love and Truth. When we speak this motto we mean that it shall operate as to all mankind. It is true that an Odd Fellow may consider and aid his fraternal brother more quickly and perhaps to a greater extent than he could a stranger. It is but natural for an enlightened human being to consider the members of his own family and to prefer them to those outside it.

Odd Fellowship does not pretend to be it religion nor a teacher of religion. It offers no substitute for the ordinary civilized code of morals Its principles are, however, those which are promulgated. and taught as the guiding rules for mankind of all religions. Odd Fellowship demonstrates exemplifies and is the proper regard for the duties each man owes to all mankind.

Odd~ Fellowship places and keeps continually before Its members clean thinking, right living examples of those whose first concern is not for themselves, but who are diligent followers of the precepts to visit the sick, bury the dead, relieve the distressed and educate the orphan. The initiate gradually comes to fully understand the meaning of these decrees and learns to follow in the footsteps of his brothers who are further 'advanced in the great work.

Herein is true Odd Fellowship and herein is the reason for the tremendous increase in strength since the inception of the Independent Order of Odd Fellows. Odd Fellowship has come to be synonymous with all that is good, right, clean, decent, generous and true. It has come to its exalted position solely through the endeavor of Odd Fellows to follow its teachings.

Chapter I
The First Odd Fellows

Compared with our present day standards, life did not hold a great deal for the average individual in the years between 1700 and 1725. Yet, then, as now, human beings were inclined to be sociable and seek the company of others. Since time immemorial it has been the custom of men to gather together and unite themselves into tribes or communities. As these tribes or communities grew there was a further alignment of families and other groups, particularly of men with the same or similar occupations or habits of life. This grouping or habit of association has given rise to our well known axioms that "Birds of a feather flock together" and "A man is known by the company he keeps."

In England, at the time mentioned, there were no clubs nor meeting places as we know them today. The only places where general assemblies of the people took place were the churches and the taverns. These taverns were the equivalent of our bar rooms. Anyone in any degree acquainted with the customs obtaining in the churches of that day will readily realize the utter impossibility of a friendly, sociable gathering in one. At the taverns, however, congenial spirits could meet and enjoy each other's company. As the average workman had little money and could go to the tavern only occasionally, it was natural that he should try to go on the night that his friends would be there.

This gradually resulted in the selection of a certain night when the entire circle of friends would make it a point to be on hand. Eventually these groups of friends formed social clubs. As time went on the clubs became more solidified and it apparently became the custom, when one of the members was ill, to take up a collection for him. Somehow the members of these clubs came to be termed Odd Fellows. Just why this name was applied or if it had some particular significance at that time does not seem to be known today. We are now equally hazy on the question as to just when this name was first attached to these organizations, but we do find a record of its being used as early as 1745.

The members of the clubs were, as a general rule, mechanics and workingmen. If one of them was out of work he traveled on foot to the next town or village. When he finally obtained employment he would go to the tavern and ascertain on what night he would meet a group of convivial townspeople, with whom he would become acquainted. After being introduced into the circle, in the town to which he had removed himself, the traveler would relate the news of his native city and tell how the club to which he belonged there operated. Naturally if the stranger brought new and worthy ideas they were adopted by the club into which he had newly come.

About the only method of communication of news in those days was by word of mouth, but information regarding these clubs spread in a surprising fashion. Although each club was formed by the initiative of its own members, each had its own rules, and the initiations; in those clubs which had initiations, were all different, the clubs began to cooperate to a surprising degree. They gradually all came to be known as Odd Fellows Lodges and, just as gradually, the members came to be known as Brothers.

Operating as they did, each under its own rules, it was inevitable that the Lodges should vary widely in their conduct. The fact has has been set forth that these Lodges were originally convivial gatherings should not be forgotten as, apparently, the main purpose of the Lodges for several years

13

was the social gathering and the good fellowship that resulted therefrom. However, as time went on, some of the Lodges began to extend their activities, some collecting dues from the members for the purpose of establishing a fund from which a Brother might derive financial aid when in distress. Others had a custom of taking up a collection for a needy Brother. Still others continued to function as they originally did, merely a meeting of friendly spirits to partake of the liquid cheer available at their meeting place, tell each other stories, and spend a happy evening with their friends.

The first writings which we have setting forth the purpose of the Lodges seem to give the ideas which had developed by the latter half of the century, probably between 1750 and 1770. They indicate that the Lodges at that time had come to be regarded as organizations of working men united for social purposes, to aid their members in obtaining employment and to assist them financially when they were in need.

It was during, or shortly before this period, that the custom of assisting Brothers to obtain employment arose. The method of operation seems to have been to furnish a Brother who was out of work with a card certifying his membership and enough money to get to the next town where there was a Lodge; if the traveler, with the assistance of the Brothers, was able to obtain employment in the town to which he had gone, he deposited his card in the Lodge and remained there. If he was unable to find work, the Brothers would furnish him money enough to go on to another town where there was a Lodge. He continued in this manner until he found employment.

Hilarity continued to be the keynote of each meeting. The meetings were still held in the taverns and the landlord, who was known as the "Host" seems to have been a sort of an official of the Lodge. Travelers became frequent and it was part of the "business" of each Lodge to call in the Host, shortly after the members had assembled, and put the inquiry: "Are there any tramps in waiting?" Some Lodges required each visitor to go through the initiation and apparently each tried to put on a little better one than the others. Everything, it seems, was considered in the initiations except the candidates' feelings and the visiting Brothers must have been stout men indeed to have endured very many of the weird and fantastic ceremonies that were performed. The idea, of course, was to provide a good time and everyone had it, except the candidates.

Chapter II
The Early Organization

Up to this point we have considered the birth and evolution of the Odd Fellows during a period when conditions in England were undergoing constant change. The Order had begun, by 1770 to attract attention. Whether we consider ancient times or our present era or any of the intervening time it has always been and is today an outstanding fact that any dictator, ruler or monarch who has been or is jealous of his power over his subjects has feared, most of all, organizations of the people. In the history of any recorded resistance to oppression the first show of unrest has displayed itself in the banding together in groups of citizens or subjects. When the American colonies revolted the English Government, which up to that time had taken no particular notice of the Odd Fellows, began a determined campaign to stamp out all secret societies. Many Lodges were disbanded and it was necessary for some time for members to conceal their connection with the Order.

It is a matter of history that George III exerted every effort to recruit troops in England, to conduct the war with the colonies in America, but was unsuccessful. He was forced to resort to the purchase of Hessians. The American Declaration of Independence had become well known in England and the phrase "life, liberty and the pursuit of happiness" had struck a popular note. There was considerable unrest in the British Isles and, although the English Government did not repeal its laws against secret societies, it relaxed the enforcement of them considerably as a matter of political expediency.

At once Odd Fellows' Lodges began to spring up. It is supposed that it was at this time that the well known policy of self institution of Lodges arose. Under this plan whenever five Brothers desired they were at liberty to start a new Lodge. The way this worked out generally was that five Brothers who lived at a distance from the Lodge or who perhaps found themselves in a city where there was no Lodge would organize and proceed to hold meetings in their own locality. The Lodge where they had been initiated was known as the "Mother" Lodge. Toward the close of the century the "Mother" Lodges began to assert a certain amount of authority over those Lodges which regarded them as the "Mother." In some cases the authority was admitted and the Lodges proceeded to work in accordance with the instructions of the "Mother" Lodge. Other Lodges denied that the "Mother" Lodge had any authority over them. The "Mother" Lodges continued to assume more and more authority and eventually began to claim authority over each other.

The word "Unity" is common in the history of Odd Fellowship and it came into use at this time. The "Mother" Lodge, and the Lodges arising as the result of efforts of its members, were termed a "Unity." There were a number of these "Unities." They were soon engaged in more or less of a "free-for-all" for supremacy of the Order. Some of them were known as the Ancient Noble Odd Fellows, the Grand United Odd Fellows, the National Odd Fellows, the Imperial Odd Fellows, and the London Unity Odd Fellows. All this time each individual Lodge was becoming more cohesive, probably as a result of the fact that they were adopting more and more the principle of mutual relief.

The battle for supremacy between these factions continued for several years. In 1813 the Lodges in the vicinity of Manchester held a convention at which several of them were represented. It was decided that the interests of the Order could best be promoted by securing general laws for the Order and uniformity in the work. The convention proposed to secure this by the organization of a governing body to be known as "The Manchester Unity of the Independent Order of Odd Fellows." In 1814 the formal organization was completed and a Grand committee (corresponding to our Grand Lodge) was provided for. This was the first stone in the solid foundation on which Odd Fellowship now rests. The committee proposed that every Lodge coming under its jurisdiction must be chartered by it. This is probably the most important difference between the Old Order and the Independent Order for it is by the issuance and the right to recall charters that Grand Lodges are now enabled to enforce obedience to their mandates.

The formation of the Manchester Unity did not end the struggle in England. Its organization however was superior to that of any other body Its method of chartering Lodges enabled it to retain control over the Lodges already subordinate to it, to institute others and keep in close contact with them. Other branches of the Order copied this system of chartering Lodges but, after several years of constant strife, the Manchester Unity finally triumphed and reigned supreme in England.

Chapter III
The First American Lodge

It was while this great contest for the position as head of the Order was going on that Thomas Wildey was initiated. He was born in London, England, on January 15, 1782, and as a boy had been apprenticed to a carriage company and learned the trade of coach spring making. Wildey became an enthusiastic worker and passed several times through the chairs. Being anxious to spread the work he, with several others, instituted Morning Star Lodge in London. Eventually stories of the opportunities available in the United States proved irresistible and Wildey landed in Baltimore, Maryland, in the late summer of 1817. Soon after his arrival here Wildey became acquainted with John Welch who was also an Englishman by birth. Welch was born in Wolverhampton in Staffordshire, England, in November, 1792. While learning the painting and plumbing trades Welch became an Odd Fellow. He came to this country shortly before Wildey, having arrived in May of 1817.

Wildey and Welch became firm friends. For some time after their arrival both were busy finding work and getting themselves established. Everything in the country being new to them there was a great deal for them to see. However, the time came when they had a little leisure and it was then they began to miss their Lodges.

The Shakespeare Grand Lodge of Odd Fellows had been organized in New York City in 1806. It continued for some time. It almost passed out of existence but was revived December 23, 1818, and after the revival continued to function until 1822. Prince Regents Lodge was instituted in New York in 1816 or thereabout. Very little is known about this Lodge and it probably was never very strong.

There was, however, no Lodge in Baltimore with which Wildey and Welch could associate themselves. As they did not know any other Odd Fellows they decided to put an advertisement in the paper. John Duncan and John Cheatham responded to the advertisement. Wildey and Welch desired to start the proposed Lodge by self institution for which it was of course necessary to have five initiates. Having secured some results from the first advertisement they decided to try again and on March 27, 1819, they inserted another advertisement in the Baltimore American, the same paper they had previously used. The notice read as follows:

NOTICE TO ODD FELLOWS

"A few members of the Society of Odd Fellows will be glad to meet their brethren for the purpose of forming a Lodge, on Friday evening, 2nd April, at the Seven Stars, Second Street, the hour of seven P. M."

Another initiate by the name of Richard Russworth responded to this advertisement. The Seven Stars was a tavern or hotel owned and operated by Thomas Lupton and it was here the members met.

The first formal meeting was held on. April 26, 1819 at which time the Brothers self-instituted themselves a Lodge which they. named Washington Lodge No. 1. This date, April 26, 1819, IS considered the natal day of American Odd Fellowship because Washington Lodge No.1 which was instituted on that date was the first Lodge which had any effectual existence over any long period of time and also because Washington Lodge No. 1 was the Lodge out of which the 1. O. O. F., as we know it today, grew.

Chapter IV
The Grand Lodge of Maryland and the United States.

John Welch, it has been noted was with Wildey, the originator of Washington Lodge. From what can be learned the idea of the formation of a Lodge was Wildey's idea and Welch was not, at first, very anxious to assist him. Welch had originally joined the Lodge in England for the fraternal association it would provide and because of its avowed purposes of mutual aid and extension of assistance to needy brothers. He was however a confirmed Church goer and a sober industrious man possessed of no convivial proclivities and was not in sympathy with the drinking and alcoholic joviality which he invariably had observed at the Lodge meetings. But when Welch did agree to join with Wildey in organizing the Lodge here he entered whole heartedly into the project. He believed, as has since been demonstrated, that the lofty ideals of the Order were such as would appeal to all men but he also believed that the atmosphere of the Lodge room as he knew it, was nothing less than a desecration of those high ideals. He therefore determined that Washington Lodge would exist on a higher moral level than the old Lodges and due undoubtedly to a great extent, to his efforts it did. Welch, more than anyone else, was responsible for the expulsion of alcohol from Odd Fellows meeting places.

As has been stated, Washington Lodge was created by self-institution in accordance with the custom of the Old Order. Immediately after the opening of the Lodge the officers were elected and installed; Thomas Wildey was the Noble Grand and John Welch the Vice Grand. These men all knew of the struggle in England for the position as head 'Of the Order. One of them, John Duncan, is reported as having been initiated into the Order in Baltimore seventeen years before the start of Washington Lodge so apparently they all knew there had been other Lodges in this country.

The first problem that faced Washington Lodge was the possibility that the same thing might happen in the United States that had happened in England, that is, a number of Lodge might spring up by self-institution and sooner or later get into an argument about which Lodge was the Grand Lodge. The most feasible way to prevent this happening was to have their Lodge declared the Grand Lodge and to assume authority right from the outset.

The Manchester Unity was advancing rapidly in England and the other so-called Independent Grand Lodges which were working under the same system, that is, issuing warrants to open Lodges, were also forging ahead. Profiting by their observation of the way matters had worked out in the Old Country the policy of Washington Lodge No.1 was changed in the first month of its existence and it was decided to thereafter continue under the work of the Independent Order. To do this it was necessary to secure a charter. The contest was still on in England and it was not yet apparent which Grand Lodge would finally emerge victorious. To be sure they had a charter from .whichever Grand Lodge came out on top, Washington Lodge applied to several of the Divisions of the Order for its charter.

During the latter part of 1819, P. G. John Crowder visited Baltimore and became acquainted with the Brothers of Washington Lodge. Crowder was a member of Duke of York Lodge, which was number seventeen in the Manchester Unity enumeration, located at Preston, England where he lived. The Brothers in Baltimore asked Crowder to petition his Lodge for a charter for them. As soon as he returned to England he did this and on February 1, 1820, the following charter was issued.

NO.   WASHINGTON'S LODGE   1

"*Pluribus Unum*"

THE GRAND LODGE OF MARYLAND, AND OF THE UNITED STATES OF AMERICA, OF THE INDEPENDENT ORDER OF ODDDFELLOWSHIP.

TO ALL WHOM IT MAY CONCERN: This WARRANT or DISPENSATION is a free gift from the Duke of York's Lodge of the Independent Order of Odd-Fellows, holden at Preston, in the County of Lancaster in Old England, to a number of brothers residing in the city of Baltimore to establish a Lodge, at the house of brother Thomas Woodward, in South Frederick street, in the said city, hailed by the title of 'No. 1 Washington Lodge, the Grand Lodge of MARYLAND and of the United States of America.' That the said Lodge, being the first established in the United States, hath power to grant a WARRANT or DISPENSATION to a number of the Independent Order of Odd-Fellowship into any State of the Union, for the encouragement and support brothers of the said Order on travel or otherwise.

And be it further observed,that the said Lodge be not removed from the house of Thomas Woodward, so long as five brothers are agreeable to hold the same.

In testimony hereof, we have subjoined our names and affixed the Seal of our Lodge, this the first day of February, one thousand eight hundred and twenty.

James Mandsley, G. M.	John Crowder. P. G.
John Cottam, N G.	W. Topping. P. G.
Geo. Nailer, V. G.	Samuel Pemberton, P. G.
John Eccles, Sec.	Geo.Ward P. G.
John Wamsley, P. G.	George Bell, P. G.
(L.S.)	(Colors)

It will be noted that in addition to styling Washington Lodge No. 1 the Grand Lodge of Maryland and of the United States, authority was given to grant a Warrant or Dispensation for the formation of other Lodges. Washington Lodge No. 1 received and formally accepted this instrument on October 23, 1820. There was now a supreme authority over Odd Fellowship in the United States. The centralization of authority, which has been in effect in this country since this first charter was received and accepted, is one of the biggest reasons for the success of the Order here. Without it such an organization as we now have would have been utterly impossible.

Shortly after the organization of Washington Lodge dissention arose among its members, the cause not now being known. With the consent of the Lodge several members withdrew and in November of 1819 organized Franklin Lodge on the principle of self-institution. Before Washington Lodge No. 1 received its Charter from Preston this Lodge made application to the Order in Manchester for a Charter. The application was not acted on until June 25, 1821, which of course was after the issuance of the Charter of Washington Lodge No. 1. The application was refused on the ground that the Charter in the possession of Washington Lodge No.1 carried with it complete and exclusive authority to issue charters for other Lodges in this country and Franklin Lodge was instructed to apply to Washington Lodge. Franklin Lodge received its Charter from Washington Lodge on August 22, 1821, and was legally and formally instituted September 5th of the same year.

While Washington Lodge was in possession of its original charter an anomalous situation existed in that it was both a Subordinate and a Grand Lodge. It was the only Lodge in the

United States legally in existence until Franklin Lodge received its charter.

It was very evident to the members of Washington Lodge that something must be done about this situation and that there must be a separate executive body completely divorced from Subordinate Lodges which should have jurisdiction over them. In 1820 a committee of Past Grands was organized, apparently with the idea that they could function in somewhat the same manner as our present Grand Lodges. While this principle was, as we have since discovered, theoretically correct, in practice it did not work as well at that time since there was no absolute authority entrusted in the committee. No actual authority had been delegated to it by Washington Lodge. Existing under those conditions its function could be only advisory.

On February 7, 1821, the Committee of Past Grands met to confer concerning the desirability of forming a Lodge to oversee the subordinate Lodges and to have actual jurisdiction over them. The only way this power could be acquired was by a surrender of the Washington Lodge Charter. Acting on a request from the Committee of Past Grands, Washington Lodge formally agreed to surrender its charter. On February 22, 1821, the charter of Washington Lodge "Which it had received from the Duke of York Lodge and which carried full and exclusive authority to issue charters to new Lodges, was surrendered to the Past Grands. They thereupon organized the Grand Lodge of Maryland and of the United States installing as its officers Thomas Wildey, Grand Master; John P. Entwisle, Deputy Grand Master; William S. Couth, Grand Warden; John Welch, Grand Secretary; John Boyd, Grand Guardian; William Larkham, Grand Conductor.

It was the intention of the newly formed Grand Lodge and the expectation of Washington Lodge, that charter would be prepared and issued at once to Washington Lodge. This charter, however, was not completed until February 9, 18222, almost a year after the surrender of the original charter by Washington Lodge. The Warrant or Dispensation when finally issued contained the following preamble:

"TO WHOM IT MAY CONCERN:

The Grand Lodge of Maryland, by authority of a Grand Charter granted from the Grand Lodge of the United States held in the City of Baltimore, State of Maryland, doth hereby grant . . ."

From this one may judge that there was apparently, even at that time, an intention that the Grand Lodge of Maryland should eventually be a separate entity, subordinate to and under the jurisdiction of a Grand Lodge of the United States. One cannot help but wonder if Wildey did not have that idea, almost from the inception of Washington Lodge. He often expressed the opinion that the Odd Fellow government should be patterned. after the government of our country and there IS a definite resemblance. The Sovereign Grand Lodge corresponds to the Federal Government; the Grand Lodges correspond to the State Governments; and the Subordinate Lodges correspond to the City Governments. As we are now able to view them, all of Wildey's efforts seem to be directed toward this end.

At the meeting of the Grand Lodge of Maryland and the United States on February 22 1821 a provision for its support was made by the adoption of a resolution providing that ten per cent of the receipts of all Subordinate Lodges should be forwarded to the Grand Lodge and in addition various other charges should be made for opening a Lodge, for the Degrees, and so forth.

Chapter V
The Growing Order

Discussions now began to take place between the Lodges and there were many When necessary to transact business other than at a regular session of the Grand Lodge, it "was the custom to call a meeting of its officer and members. This group was entitled the 'Grand Committee." Actions of the Grand Committee were vested with the full authority of the Grand Lodge only after they were approved by the Grand Lodge at a regular meeting. The Grand Committee met on April 13, 1823, and granted an application from Massachusetts Lodge No. 1 for a charter, and also granted a dispensation for a Grand Lodge empowered to charter other Lodges within that State. Grand Master Wildey was selected to take the documents to Boston. This he did, instituting the Subordinate Lodge on June 9th, 1823, and the Grand Lodge on June 11th of the same year.

While on his way to Boston, Wildey visited Columbia Lodge No.1 at New York City. This Lodge had received a dispensation from Loyal Beneficent Duke of Sussex Lodge No.2 at Liverpool, which was another of the Lodges attempting to establish its authority as the Supreme Lodge of England. Wildey persuaded these brethren that it would be advantageous for them and beneficial to the Order for them to apply to the Grand Lodge of Maryland and of the United States for a charter. The Grand Committee convened on June 15, 1823, to consider the application of Columbia Lodge. The application was granted and the charter so promptly forwarded that on his way back from Boston, Grand Master Wildey was enabled on June 24, 1823, to institute the Lodge and install the officers.

On this trip to Boston, Wildey had also stopped at Philadelphia where there was a self-instituted Lodge. He induced this Lodge (Pennsylvania No. 1) to make application to the Grand Lodge of Maryland and of the United States for a charter. The application for a charter was approved and the charter together with one for a Grand Lodge prepared. On his return from Boston, Wildey again went to Philadelphia and on June 27, 1823, instituted both Pennsylvania Lodge No. 1 and the Grand Lodge of Pennsylvania.

Chapter VI
The Grand Lodge of the United State

There were indications of a feeling that all Grand Lodges should be on an equal footing. It became evident that the only way to insure harmony within the Order was to separate the Grand Lodge of Maryland and the Grand Lodge of the United States. This would leave the Grand Lodge of Maryland authority over the Subordinate Lodges in the State, which would be equivalent to the authority of other Grand Lodges in their respective jurisdictions. In the Grand Lodge of the United States was to be vested' authority over all Grand Lodges with equal representation from all Grand Lodges.

This proposal was brought up at the regular meeting of the Grand Lodge held February 22, 1824, at which meeting each Grand Jurisdiction was represented by a member or proxy. After the recess of the Grand Lodge, the Grand Committee met and adopted a resolution requiring the representative of each Grand Jurisdiction to communicate with his constituents and determine their feeling with regard to the proposed Grand Lodge of the United States. As all approved, a committee was appointed to prepare a Constitution. On November 22, 1824, the Grand Lodge of Maryland and of the United States convened. This was its last session in its dual capacity. From that time on it was recognized as the Grand Lodge of Maryland with only the usual Grand Lodge authority.

At a preliminary meeting on January 15, 1825, for the purposes of the organization of the Grand Lodge of the United States, a Constitution was adopted subject to approval by the Grand Lodges of the several jurisdictions. Among other provisions in the original constitution was one that Baltimore, Maryland was to be the "permanent" seat of the Grand Lodge of the United States. As finally adopted September 25, 1825, the word "present" was substituted for "permanent" in this section so that it read: "The present seat of the Grand Lodge of the United States shall be at Baltimore, Maryland."

By the end of the year of 1825, there were four Grand Lodges in existence: the Grand Lodge of Maryland meeting at Baltimore, with three subordinate Lodges; the Grand Lodge of Pennsylvania meeting at Philadelphia, with three subordinate Lodges; the Grand Lodge of Massachusetts meeting at Boston, with two subordinate Lodges; and the Grand Lodge of New York meeting at New York, with one subordinate.

At this time four Degrees were used in addition to the intermediate degrees. The fourth was known as the Golden Rule Degree. This Degree was conferred only on Past Grands. The intermediate Degrees were called Covenant and Remembrance. It was apparently during this year that the Patriarchal Degree was brought over from England and first conferred in this country.

During the year 1826, Grand Master Wildey visited in England to determine whether or not there was anything new in the workings of the Order. Before his departure from England, he was presented with a new Charter by the Duke of York Lodge which confirmed the privileges granted by the original charter and reaffirmed them to the "Grand Lodge of America." The new charter was granted by the Grand Annual Moveable Committee, which was the supreme authority of the Manchester Unity.

By the end of 1826, the number of subordinate Lodges in this country had increased to twelve. No new Grand Lodges had been chartered.

Charter VII
The First Encampment-- The Separation from the English Order

The Patriarchal Degree originated in England but the Royal Purple Degree is believed to be of American origin. It was probably the work of John P. Entwisle, the author of the Covenant and Remembrance Degrees. Entwisle was a native born Englishman. He was educated for the ministry but preferred newspaper work and was well and favorably known in this line of work. Entwisle was elected Grand Secretary in 1823. It is to him that credit is due for the adoption by the Grand Lodge of the United States of the first system of representation.

Just what the restrictions as to the conferring of the Patriarchal and Royal Purple Degrees first were IS not now clear. On May 6, 1827, Wildey and several other brethren met and decided on the organization of a higher Lodge to confer the Patriarchal, Royal Purple and also the Golden Rule Degree. Only Scarlet Degree members of the Order were to be eligible. They petitioned the Grand Lodge of Maryland for a charter to open an "Encampment Lodge." The charter was granted and Encampment Lodge No. 1 instituted July 6, 1827. The first charter was lost and a new one Issued January 16, 1829. This charter carried full and exclusive authority to establish Encampment Lodges anywhere on the globe. Under its authority another encampment was opened in Maryland and one in Delaware.

In other States, the Grand Lodges were petitioned for Charters to open Encampment. They granted these and shortly the Grand Lodges required their members to be in posession of the Encampment Degrees. In 1829 the Grand Lodge of Pennsylvania authorized the establishment of a Grand Encampment and other Grand Jurisdictions followed suit.

The Grand Lodge of the United States continued its work under the constitution of 1825, until the session held in September of 1833, at which time a new constitution was adopted. It was much more verbose than the original one, but contained only two important changes or additions :First, the name of the organization was definitely fixed by entitling the Grand Lodge of the United States in the new Constitution a "The Grand Lodge of the Independent Order of Odd Fellows of the United States of America;" and second that its jurisdiction was described as being co-extensive with the Federal Government of the United States. The jurisdiction was further extended by the statement, "This Grand Lodge has inherent power to establish Lodges in Foreign Countries where no Grand Lodge exists." This was the first definite assertion of an assumption of authority by the Grand Lodge beyond that delegated to it by the two charters it had received.

At the Grand Lodge session of 1835, the discontent with the Order as it existed in England was first actually expressed. Perhaps it would be more correct to say the dissatisfaction was with the practices of the members of the Order in England. At this session Representative Ridgely of Maryland offered a resolution requiring the committee on correspondence to write a letter to the brethren in Great Britain, congratulating them on the state of the Order in that Country and respectfully suggesting to them "the propriety of discontinuing all convivial practices in their Lodges."

As before noted the Grand Lodge of the United States had already taken unto itself, in the Constitution of 1833, authority to establish Lodges in foreign countries where no Grand

Lodge was in existence. This was an assumption of authority beyond that extended by the charter received from England in 1826, and, it would seem, amounted to a Declaration of Independence by the Grand Lodge of the United States. This matter never did become, as might have been expected, a subject of contention between the Supreme Lodges in the two countries. The break, when it did come, was due, more than anything else, to a desire on the part of American Odd Fellows to establish more firmly the respectable reputation they already had earned themselves and their Lodges and to discontinue associations no matter how remote with anything that might discredit them or be subject to reproach.

Not only was there dissatisfaction with the condition of the Order in England but there was also some dissension in the United States and the Lodges were given to a limited amount of quarreling among themselves.

At the session of 1836, the Grand Lodge of the United States, because of differences between the Lodges in New York State, ordered the charter of the Grand Lodge of New York revoked, to be restored by the Committee on the State of New York only when harmony was regained in that . jurisdiction. The charter was revoked May 22, 1837. It was restored November 23, 1837.

The system of allowing Grand Lodges to issue charters for Grand Encampment led to more or less trouble and confusion. The Grand Lodge of he United States had issued a charter for a Grand Encampment in Maryland in 1831. In 1841, it withdrew the right of State Grand Lodges to charter Grand Encampments. From this time on he Grand Lodge of the United States issued all charters for Grand Encampments. By constitutional amendment the Grand Lodge of the United States admitted representatives of the Grand Encampments to membership on September 21, 1841. This step placed the Encampments on an equal basis with the Subordinate Lodges.

At the annual session of 1842, the differences between the Order in the United States and Great Britain had become so great that they could be overlooked no longer. Two commissioners had been appointed for the purpose of arbitration and had gone to England to try to reunite the two Orders but the rift between them had widened into too great a chasm to be bridged. By formal resolution in 1843, all ties between the 1. O. O. F. and the Manchester Unity were severed.

At the session of 1843, a petition for a Lodge at Hamburg, Germany, was presented. The petition was not in regular form. It, therefore, was ordered that a charter be issued upon receipt of a proper application. This was the first petition for a charter for a Lodge in a foreign country received by The Grand Lodge of the United States.

Charter VIII
The Rebekahs

The first mention of women in the Order was made in 1845, at the annual session of the Grand Lodge when the following resolution was presented:

"RESOLVED, That each Subordinate Lodge may, by a vote of two-thirds of its members voting, grant a card to a wife of any member who may apply for it, signed by the officers of the Lodge, and countersigned by the recipient on the margin, and to remain in force not more than one year, and that similar cards may be granted to the widows of Odd Fellows, to remain in force as long as they remain such."

That there was opposition to the intrusion of women in any way or form was evidenced by the vote on this resolution which, as can be seen, did not give any rights whatsoever to the holder of such a card. The vote was close-twenty-three for the resolution and twenty-one against it.

At the session of 1847 Grand Sire Shulock reported that a charter had been sent to The Grand Lodge of British North America which had jurisdiction over all of Canada, by which a separate and distinct sovereignty was almost treated, the said Lodge being placed on a footing nearly equal that of the Grand Lodge of the United States. It was at this (1847) session that the first agitation for revision of the organization of State Grand Lodges occurred. Up to this time all Past Grands were eligible and could vote. It was proposed that hereafter representation in State Grand Lodges should be on a proportionate basis as in the Grand Lodge of the United States so as to give each Lodge proportionate representation. Heretofore, all the Past Grands in the city where the Grand Lodge was held would attend while the distant Lodges could send only a few because of the expense. The result was to give the Lodges in the city where the Grand Lodge was held control of it by the more numerous vote. Article X of the constitution was amended to provide for the election of Representatives for a term of two years.

At the regular annual session held in Cincinnati in September of 1850, the question of affiliating women with the Lodge again came to the front and a legislative committee reported on the matter. The proposition as first put forth, intended the establishment of an Honorary Degree for the wives and daughters of Scarlet Degree members and also an Honorary Degree for the wives and daughters of Past Officers. Reporting, Representatives J. C. La Rue and J. A. Kennedy of the Committee recommended that the institution of such Degrees would be inappropriate and inopportune. Representative Schuyler Colfax of Indiana, the third member of the committee, rendered a minority report in which he concurred in the recommendation against a separate Special Degree for wives and daughters of Past Officers, but differed from the majority of the committee in regard to a Special Degree for wives of Scarlet Degree members. Therefore, after listing several good and logical reasons, he presented the following.

> "RESOLVED, That a Special Committee of three members be appointed to prepare an appropriate Honorary Degree, with an accompanying Sign or Signs and Passwords, to be conferred upon the wives of Scarlet Degree members who are in good standing in the Order, and that such Committee report such degree for consideration at the next Communication of this Grand Lodge."

Naturally, the minority report, when presented with so many

37

sound reasons why it should be accepted, evoked a great deal of discussion. After much argument the minority report was finally, on September 20, 1850, adopted. Representatives Colfax, Martin of Mississippi, and Steele of Tennessee, were appointed a committee to prepare the Degree. Their report was submitted and one year later, September 20, 1851, the "Female" (Rebekah) Degree was adopted as an Honorary Degree by the Grand Lodge of the United States. The Degree, as reported, could be bestowed on all Scarlet Degree members and their wives. In 1852, a decision of Grand Sire Moore that the officers of all Lodges ought to be in regular possession of the Rebekah Degree, was approved. It was also decided at this meeting that the Degree of Rebekah could be, under certain conditions, conferred on the widow of a Scarlet Degree member.

It is not surprising that the Rebekah Degree was prepared in the thorough, efficient and beautiful manner in which it was first presented when we bear in mind that Schuyler Colfax was the author of it. He was loved and trusted in the Order, and that he was loved and trusted outside it too is evidenced by the high positions in public life to which he was raised and which he so honestly and efficiently filled. Colfax was undoubtedly Odd Fellowship's greatest orator. He probably addressed more members of the Order than any other man ever did. The greatest tribute that can be paid him, and the one which he probably would have appreciated most, is to say that at all times, in sickness and health, in prosperity and adversity, in joy and sorrow, in public life and in private he was a true Odd Fellow. The Order may well be proud to have claimed him, as it did, from his initiation until he was laid in his final resting place by the tender and loving hands of his sorrrowing brothers. Any member of any branch of the Order may well honor Schuyler Colfax and feel that he is honoring one to whom honor is justly due.

Charter IX
The Golden Age-- The Patriarchs Militant-- Home of the Order

From the session of 1852 until the session of 1856, little of great importance occurred in the Order. There was, it is true, some disappointment with its functioning in Vermont, and it became necessary to withdraw the charter of the Grand Lodge of British North America. As a result, the Lodges in Canada reverted to the jurisdiction of the Grand Lodge of the United States. The situation as a whole, however, was one to instill a happy contentment in the heart of any Brother. Lodges and Encampments were springing up everywhere, practically all of them meeting with success. Each session of the Grand Lodge of the United States granted a few charters for Grand Lodges and Grand Encampments and then after listening to reports filled with practically nothing but good news, adjourned and went home.

At the session of 1856, it was decided that members of the Rebekah Degree might organize for the promotion of benevolence. Although this matter was not considered of great importance at the time, subsequent events have shown that it was one of the most momentous acts of any Grand Lodge of the United States. This was the entering wedge of our present Rebekah Lodges.

In 1857, Grand Sire Ellison rendered his report. In speaking of the Order, he said: "It is not in those far off islands of the sea, where the standard of Odd Fellowship waves in triumph, or by the rivers of Oregon, whose. tumbling waters give voice to desolation, nor m the far distant Territorial possessions. of .the West that we must look for a decline in interest or in numerical strength, but in the populous States, where it is an easy matter to be an Odd Fellow; where social life and social pleasures, in their never ending variety, the natural concomitants of a crowded population, draw us almost imperceptibly from the quiet retreat of .the Lodge room and its healthy influences, until indifference. and neglect, like base rust which consumes solid iron, will contract our resources and our means for doing good." It would seem as though Grand Sire Ellison had the gift of prophecy. It is more true at the present time than ever before that we must guard ourselves against those thugs of which he warned us.

The session of 1861 was a dark and gloomy proceeding. The clouds of war had cast their shadow on the land. Grand Sire Boylston of South Carolina, together with thirty representatives from eleven jurisdictions South and South West of Maryland were absent. Resolutions were introduced and passed that all political differences should be left outside the Lodge rooms. The appearance of Past Grand Sire Wildey at this session of the Grand Lodge of the United States was his last. He died just a month later (October 19, 1861) in his eightieth year.

Like the preceding session the meeting of the Grand Lodge in 1862 was marked by gloom tending almost to despondency. However, the general condition of affairs in the Order was much better than was to be expected. The deaths of P. G. S. Thomas Wildey and P. G. S. Horn Kneass were reported and resolutions expressing the deepest affection for them and. regret at their passing were adopted. A committee to plan the erection of a suitable memorial to Wildey was appointed. 'The action of this committee eventually resulted m the construction of the Wildey monument in Baltimore. At this session a communication from A. L. Hill, G. M. of Virginia, was received. This reminded the session that mail could still be dispatched to the jurisdictions whose representatives were proscribed by military regulations from attending. Copies of all proceedings were sent to all the Grand Lodges unable to be represented.

The most joyous session the Grand Lodge of the United States had ever known was opened in Baltimore on September 18, 1865. A full complement of representatives from the South was on hand to take the chairs which had been reserved for them since hostilities first forced their absence. The cornerstone of the Wildey monument had been laid by Grand Sire Veitch on April 26 1865, and, after a magnificent procession the elaborate structure was accepted and dedicated by the Grand Lodge.

The meetings from 1865 to 1875 were as a rule, quiet and without any far reaching results. The Order was in good condition and, in practically every locality, expanding and prospering. The most Important event during this period took place when the session of 1869 adopted a resolution authorizing each jurisdiction to prepare and adopt a form of charter suitable for Rebekah Degree Lodges. Membership in the Rebekah Degree ad in 1868 been extended to take in widows of Odd Fellows who had not received the Scarlet Degree.

At the sessions of 1872 and 1873, resolutions were promulgated concerning the wearing of a uniform by the Encampment members. In 1874, in response to a repeated and clamorous demand, an elaborate uniform for the Patriarchal Branch was prescribed by the Grand Lodge.

The Grand Lodge convened in Philadelphia on September 18, 1876, while the Centennial Exhibition was in progress. One day, being set apart as "Odd Fellows Day", the Grand Lodge and other members of the Order staged what was, at that time, undoubtedly the largest procession ever witnessed in the city. Seventeen thousand five hundred and sixty men divided into twenty divisions with ninety-two brass bands and nine fife and drum corps paraded. The line of march was crowded with visitors to the exhibition from all over the country and the demonstration itself was undoubtedly the best and, quite likely, the most effective advertising the Order had ever had.

The invitation of the Grand Lodge to Austin, Texas for the meeting in 1878 had been accepted but on the appearance of yellow fever there, the acceptance was withdrawn by Grand Sire Stokes and the meeting held in Baltimore. At this meeting the Rebekahs were granted the use of an annual password and the privilege of membership was extended to daughters of Scarlet Degree members above the age of eighteen.

In 1879 the constitution of the Grand Lodge of the United States was altered and the word "sovereign" inserted so that the title now was "The Sovereign Grand Lodge of the Independent Order of Odd Fellows." At this session it was decided that a member of a subordinate Lodge who had received the Rebekah Degree was not entitled to the Rebekah semi-annual password unless he was a member in good standing of a Rebekah Lodge. This was the final stroke of legislation needed to put the Rebekahs on a solid footing.

The session of 1880 seems to have been inconsequential in its results but the meeting in Cincinnati in 1881 produced legislation which has had a far reaching and lasting effect on the Order. It was called to the attention of the representatives that there had been an attempt to form an association to be known as "The Patriarchal Circle" which was to be composed only of Odd Fellows. Its purpose was to promulgate several new Degrees for uniformed patriarchs. This movement was effectively blocked for the time beeing, although a certain amount of difficulty was later experienced with it. A resolution was adopted prohibiting membership by an Odd Fellow in any organization using any of the emblems or devices of Odd Fellowship which had not been approved by the Sovereign Grand Lodge. The proponents of this movement did not, however, give up without a struggle and the final result of their efforts was the formation of the Patriarchs Militant.

A revised ritual was adopted to take effect July 1 1882. Under this enactment all work of the Subordinate Lodges must be done in the Third Degree. The Initiatory Degree remained as it was but the five Subordinate Lodge Degrees were contracted into three to be known as the "Pink," "Blue" and "Scarlet." Upon the adoption of this work the apron disappeared from the regalia of Subordinate Lodges.

The Patriarchal Circle was still a thorn in the side of the Sovereign Grand Lodge at its meeting in 1885. The Uniformed Degree Camps were growing rapidly.

Whether it was in response to their demands or a matter of expediency and a thrust at the "Circle" is not clear. At this session a revision of their work was approved and the Degree renamed the Patriarchs Militant. As usual the Rebekahs were present with a request and at this session a committee was appointed to revise the Ritual of their Degree. This committee reported at the session of 1886 and the revised ritual was adopted to take effect January 1, 1887. By its provisions the wife, unmarried daughter, unmarried sister, the mother (if a widow), and the unmarried step-daughter of an Odd Fellow were declared eligible to membership.

While in Denver in 1887 the Sovereign Grand Lodge

authorized Subordinate Grand Lodges to provide for the founding and maintenance of homes for the needy and helpless members of the Order or those to whom the assistance of the Order was due. This was the initial legislation on this subject. The maintenance of the numerous beautiful and commodious homes is one of the most important functions of the Order today. The construction of them was made possible by this Act. At the session of 1888 Grand Sire White spoke very strongly in favor of the organization of such homes.

In 1889 the first National Convention of delegates from Rebekah Lodges was held. Their suggestions, petitions, prayers and complaints to the Sovereign Grand Lodge were so numerous that it was necessary to appoint a special committee on the Degree of Rebekah to receive them. It was probably to escape being buried in another such deluge that the law permitting the holding of national Rebekah conventions was repealed in 1890 although the State assemblies were still to be continued.

The reports at the session of 1891 indicated a prosperous condition of the Order so it was decided to hold the next meeting in 1892 at Portland, Oregon, which was done at very large expense.

In 1893, alarmed by the enormous debt being incurred by the Patriarchs Militant, this branch of the Order was placed under the control of the various Grand Encampments. At the next session a new code for the regulation of the Rebekahs was adopted which provided that all Rebekah officers should be women.

In 1895, the constitution was amended to provide that "no saloon-keeper, bar-tender or professional gambler shall be eligible to membership in this Order." This was a big step forward for the Order and one which, considering the fact that in small towns the saloon-keepers were generally gentlemen with a great deal of prestige, it must have taken a great deal of courage for the Sovereign Grand Lodge to take. At the same session the purchase of an office and Grand Lodge building in Baltimore was voted.

In 1896, a new ritual for Rebekah Lodges was adopted and the Encampment regalia was changed. The new ritual did not prove at all satisfactory and in 1897 it was completely revised.

For a long period of time the Sovereign Grand Lodge continued to hold its annual meetings without anything which vitally affected the Order occurring. There was always, of course, a certain mount of legislation to be passed and the usual number of routine duties. Each session listened to the report of the Grand Sire and the Grand Secretary and heard of increases in memberships in the Subordinate Lodges, Rebekahs, Encampments and Patriarchs Militant, and increase in the numbers of the Lodges and Grand Jurisdictions. A new ritual for subordinate Lodges was adopted in 1907 to take effect July 1, 1908. At the session of 1908 a new and improved Rebekah Ritual was adopted in 1911; it was reported that the total membership of the Order had passed the two million mark!

The years during which the World War was being waged were not particularly eventful ones for the Order. Gains in numerical strength continued to be shown. The entire membership was committed to do its utmost for general war relief and in 1918 the Sovereign Grand Lodge set aside $ 75,000.00 for this purpose.

In 1921, endowments for the homes maintained y the Order

were sanctioned. At this session a committee was appointed to inquire into the desirability of the institution of a juvenile branch of the Order. They reported in favor of this proposition in 1922 whereupon another committee was appointed to prepare a suitable ritual.

Chapter X
The Rebekah Assembly -- The Junior Branch -- The Ladies Auxiliary -- The Education Foundation -- The Theta Rho Girls

It will be recalled that the National Conventions of Rebekahs had been discontinued. A national Rebekah Assembly which was a purely voluntary organization had been formed. It had been meeting for several years and had to a great extent replaced the conventions. It was proposed that the Sovereign Grand Lodge charter the Assembly. This was done in 1922, the Assembly thereafter being under the jurisdiction of the Sovereign Grand Lodge. The big majority voting in favor of this action is easily explained. A great many delegates to the Assembly were wives of Representatives. In the interests of domestic peace the Representatives just had to favor the measure. There is also the fact to be considered that, approved or un approved, the ladies were going to meet anyway so they might as well be sanctioned. The Assembly has, ever since its inception, been a very capable body. Since being officially recognized, it has rendered very meritorious service to the Sovereign Grand Lodge.

The special committee on the juvenile branch of the Order reported in 1923. The committee members were Thomas T. Warham of Minnesota, Karl C. Brueck of California, W. F. Jackson of Kansas and W. L. Hamilton of Ontario. They presented a bill creating a Junior Branch, a code of laws to govern it and a ritual and secret work to be used by it. Special credit was given Brother J. J. Stotler of Kansas City who had organized a boy's club in connection with this Lodge. This club had been functioning very well and their appearance in Detroit, where they had put on their work for the Sovereign Grand Lodge in 1922, had done much to swing sentiment in favor of a Junior Branch. The report of the committee was adopted and the bills relating thereon were, after minor amendments, passed.

In furtherance of the work among young people, the Association of Rebekah Assemblies was empowered in 1926 to establish an educational foundation. A committee was appointed to inquire into the workings of other such organizations. The committee rendered a favorable report at the meeting in 1927. Acting on the committtee's recommendations laws were enacted creating the Educational Foundation of the I. O. O. F. and providing for its expenses and manner of operation. The Ladies Auxiliary of the Patriarchs Militant was also created at the same (1926) meeting.

The Lodge departments had now become many and varied. There were the Subordinate Lodges, . Encampments, and Patriarchs Militant for the husbands and fathers, the Rebekahs and Ladies Auxiliaries for the wives and mothers and the Juvenile Branch for the sons. Obviously some place in the Order should be found for the daughters. In 1929, a committee was appointed to investigate the feasibility of forming a junior branch for girls. At the session of 1930 the Committee reported back that they had reached no conclusions and asked to be continued for a year which request was granted. In 1931, a new' Article and Chapter was added to the Sovereign Grand Lodge code of laws providing for the formation and regulation of the Theta Rho girls. This completed the circle. The entire family was now privileged to do its part for the Order.

Charter XI
Conclusion

From the inauspicious beginning Order has grown until today "the sun never sets on its domain." In addition to the Grand Lodges in the forty-eight States there are Gand Lodges in Alberta, British Columbia, District of Columbia, Manitoba, Maritime Provinces, Ontario, Quebec and Saskatchewan.

The quasi-independent jurisdictions are Australia, Asia, Czecho-Slovakia, Denmark, Latin America, Netherlands, Norway, Poland Sweden and Switzerland.

Subordinate Lodges immediately under the jurisdiction of the Sovereign Grand Lodge are located in the Argentine Republic, Hawaii (2) Japan, Mexico (2) Panama (2) and the Philippine Islands (2).

The Order maintains sixty-five homes for the aged and infirm members and for the widows and orphans of members. The value of these homes is between fifteen and sixteen million dollars. In addition there are many trusts, the income of which is used for the aid or support of members.

The impossibility of details in regard the Order in a small space is demonstrated by the fact that nearly six million persons have been initiated into it. These members have expended **approximately three hundred million dollars of which there is record** for the relief of suffering and distress. Of the amount spent in a like manner, of which there is no record, it would be impossible to make an estimate.

There were in existence in 1934 thirteen thousand five hundred seventy-eight Subordinate Lodges and nine thousand five hundred Rebekah Lodges. There were three thousand and thirty-one Subordinate Encampments, sixty-eight Junior Lodges, one hundred four Theta Rho Girls Clubs and six hundred ninety-seven Cantons Patriarchs Militant. The depression has caused a large decrease in these figures but it is expected that the year 1935 will show a large increase in all of these figures.

The Independent Order of Odd Fellows has been in existence for one hundred sixteen years since the time Thomas Wildey and his group of hardy pioneers instituted Washington Lodge No. 1. Each year has seen improvement; each year has seen a more solidified growth; each year has seen the advancement necessary to keep step with the growing needs of an enlightened civilization. The Odd Fellows, while aspiring to the stars, have kept their feet on solid ground; while appealing most to man's spiritual nature they have not forgotten that he has physical needs. They have assisted their Brothers when in need, and have looked after and cared for his widow and orphans.

Only a sincere Odd Fellow can fully appreciate the privilege accorded him when he was permitted to associate himself with the Order.

Suggested Reading List

Alexrod, Alan. *The International Encyclopedia of Secret Societies and Fraternal Orders.* New York: Checkmark / Facts on File, 1997.

Beharrell, Thomas G. *The Brotherhood: Being a Presentation of the Principles of Odd Fellowship.* Indianapolis: The Brotherhood Publishing, 1874.

Carnes, Mark C. *Secret Ritual and Manhood in Victorian America.* New Haven CT : Yale University Press, 1989

Christy, Frank S. *Six Links of Fellowship : Sovereign Grand Lodge Sessions in California.* NP : Grand Lodge of California, 1995.

Code of General Law of the Independent Order of Odd Fellows (Annotated). Baltimore: The Sovereign Grand Lodge, 1915.

Curry, Elvin J. *The Red Blood of Odd Fellowship.* Baltimore : Published by the author, 1903.

Dodge, Francis M. *The Story of Odd Fellowship.* Highland Park MI : Privately printed, 1935

Emery, George and Emery, J. C. Herbert. *A Young Man's Benefit : The Independent Order of Odd Fellows and Sickness Insurance in the United States of America and Canada 1860 – 1929.* Montreal, ONT : McGill-Queen's University Press, 1999

Ferguson, Charles W. *Fifty Million Brothers.* New York: Farrer & Rinehart, 1937.

Franco, Barbara. "Many Fraternal Groups Grew From Masonic Seed (Part 1 — 1730-1860)" *The Northern Light* September 1985 (Pages 4-8)

Greer, John Michael. *The Element Encyclopedia of Secret Societies and Hidden History*. New York: Barnes and Nobles, 2006

Greer, John Michael, [editor] *The Emblems of Odd Fellowship*. NP: Fir Mountain Press, 1998

Greer, John Michael, [editor]. *The Ancient Ritual of the Order of Patriotic Odd Fellows, 1797*. NP: Fir Mountain Press, 1998

Journal of the Proceedings of the Seventy-First Annual Session of the Grand Lodge. Independent Order of Odd Fellows of Michigan. Lansing: R Smith, 1915.

Ridgeley, James L. *History of American Odd Fellowship: The First Decade*. Baltimore: The Grand Lodge, 1878.

Ritual of A Lodge of Odd Fellows under the Jurisdiction of the Sovereign Grand Lodge of the Independent Order of Odd Fellows. Revised edition. NP : Sovereign Grand Lodge, 2004

Ritual of a Junior Lodge under the Jurisdiction of the Sovereign Grand Lodge of the Independent Order of Odd Fellows. Revised 1958. NP:Sovereign Grand Lodge, 1958

Ross, Theodore A. *The Official and Legal History and Manual of Odd Fellowship*. New York: M. W. Hansen, 1899.

Smith, Don R. [Compiler] *The Three Link Fraternity : Odd Fellowship in California : An Introduction to the Independent*

Order of Odd Fellows and Rebekahs. NP: Grand Lodge of California, 1993.

Stallings, J. Edward [Compiler]. *The Dreams of the Founding Fathers* NP: Privately Printed, ND.

Stallings, J. Edward [Compiler]. *The Grand Sires.* NP : Privately Printed,, ND.

Stallings, J. Edward [Compiler]. *Searching for Treasures.* NP : Privately Printed, ND.

Tabbert, Mark A. "The Odd Fellows", *The Northern Light,* Dec 2003

Whalen, William J. *Handbook of Secret Organizations.* Milwaukee: Bruce Publishing, 1966.

Made in the USA
Columbia, SC
27 August 2020